METAL, HEAVY

By Micah D. Zevin

Poets of Queens Press
New York, 2020

Designed and composed by Oleksandr Fraze-Frazenko.

On the Cover:
Photo by Harry Cunningham.
Design by Oleksandr Fraze-Frazenko.

© All rights reserved. Printed in the USA. No part of this work may be reproduced or used in any form by any means — graphic, electronic or mechanical, including photocopying, recording, taping or usage in information storage and retrieval systems — without prior written permission of the authors, except for brief extracts for the purpose of review of this book.

ISBN 978-1-7351478-1-9

CONTENTS

SIDE I: Spirits 8
    Attitude 8
    The Shadow You 10
    The Stone Steps Into an Open Field and Goes Unnoticed 11
    Spirits, Before 12
    Spirits, After 13
    Spirits, Heavy and Metal 14
    Speed Up and Open Your Eyes Before You Miss the Surprise 15

SIDE II: Concept Album 16
    New Dimensions Straddle Two Worlds 17
    The Subway 18
    Real Life 19
    Far Beyond Memory 20
    Wishing I May Have Might 21
    Puzzles in Hidden Cities 22
    Tool Poem #3 23
    Them Bones: 24
    An Indirect Alice in Chains Tribute 24
    Concept Album 25
    Personification: Extinction Chronicles 26

SIDE III: Interrogations 28
    Lobster Girl, I Feel Bad for You: A Metal Poem 29
    Sad Donut! 30
    My Wounds Have a Message; The Toxic Truth Soothsayer 31
    In the Theater of My Dreams 33
    Gravitas, an Oval Shape 34
    The Non-Non Place 35
    Interrogations of Selves 36

SIDE IV: Documents 38
    Document #15: The Present Future Past 39
    Document #12: The Dance 40
    A Manual for Hope and Nightmares 41
    Conflicting Sirens 42
    Document #5: Signs of Life (Unstuck in Time) 43
    Used for Parts 44
    Viral Days (Daze) 45
    Metal, Heavy 46
    Document #16: The Fine Line or Living in America 47

*Thanks to my wife, Holly,
for her love and support
on this continued creative journey.*

SIDE 1:
SPIRITS

Attitude

I think my guinea pig Salty has a Heavy Metal Punk Rock attitude. She bites and guinea
pigs are not supposed to bite although she did come from a conventional pet store that is now out of business. Outwardly, she is the alpha and she dominates her cage sister Peppa or Pep, and she likes to climb on her pig mom, on my wife's shoulders, and dive bombs off in a cardboard box specially set up with a blanket that we grab and ready on the couch below. She's a badass bully pig who likes to run, jump and jig. Her wild tufts of orange black white fur make her appear as if she is always ready to head bang or rock until it's
time to nap or eat lettuce again.

THE SHADOW YOU

Waking up in the dark is eerie
but not as eerie as the news.
It's an assault on the senses, an echo
that never seems to stop bouncing off
the walls of caverns.
When you are perpetually tired,
you forget yourself
escalating aches, pains and blockages
that lead(s) to dwindling options, ambitions.
Am I am becoming a stranger to and in
my own body?
Am I a cloud hovering
over myself in humid air
about to burst with rain?
When operating partly in the dark
you must find a high-powered flashlight
to navigate the forest and
find your way home,
if you have a home.
Oh Mockingbird!
Every breath I take,
you are burrowing into my bones
until I pray to be in fine hands
to move to another land
where life is not only a stage
and you are turning
the now browning pages.
There are no thrones for
me to sit on nor things or
people I have ever called marvelous.
Live from jokes about reunification
and peace
I am greeted by a nation's dismantling sanity,
the crowds in and outside my mind
trying to avoid high stakes missions
instead to be persuaded
that all I can do or desire to do
is play it safe.

THE STONE STEPS INTO AN OPEN FIELD AND GOES UNNOTICED

The lightning hits the ground like an apocalyptic symphony.
Everyone on the farm scatters for shelter, including the animals.
The stone is the only one to go unscathed and avoid
the terror of the alien force trying to eliminate human, plant, animal.
The next morning, there are holes in houses and banks.
Only cars made of heavy metals require no immediate work.
The stone is a marker for all beginnings and endings.
The bunny rabbit sits on a warm surface in the morning light
waiting for its prey to rise out of slumber
and run as it smells the gravity of birds circling their tiny heads.
In the forest the stone is next to a tree or covered by foliage.
Humans hide behind it silent as bark to hunt deer
in camouflage; some say the stone is what makes the sorcerer.
The illustrator draws magic with their hands to bring the inanimate
to life.

SPIRITS, BEFORE

The ghosts are boasting about their enduring embraces.
The ghosts demand more company
are tired of stalking
sleeping faces.
The ghosts yearn for the days they exceeded
at bowling and could bowl you over with
laughter.
The ghosts think any love is a strange love
because there is a god up above, because there is a
god up above?

SPIRITS, AFTER

Does red wine have a connection to strange love?
From a time when you drank libations from a
enormous silver glass just like in *Game of Thrones*
so much so that it gets all over your face and
you appear like you're lusting after blood
like a vampire. This is both gothic and heavy metal.
I make beef stir-fry and it marinates in oyster sauce,
vinegar, sesame oil and sweet chili sauce. This brings
me compliments and sometimes kisses laced with
Pinot Noir. My wife is exhausted by the nonsense
of the week.

SPIRITS, HEAVY AND METAL

Am I becoming a ghost or am I
chasing my mortality
through the darkness of nights
where I cannot sleep, instead
listening to the drunk wolves
screaming like banshees in
desperation as they fumble
to their destinations,
if they have one.
Are ghosts real or a bag of bones
or simply human beings dressed
in black and white makeup to
evoke existence beyond and
outside the body, time, playing
church organs, electric guitars,
operatic, lyrics both right and wrong,
singing hauntings into your headphones
as you ride on bus or subway?
In fantasy movie worlds, heavy metals
coalesce around your body and mind
like liquid ooze coming off T2 from Terminator 2—
who like a ghost takes the form of a man,
seemingly out of nowhere, and
stabs you with their long knife shaped arm
of martial law unlike Arnold Schwarzenegger's
first Terminator, who seemed to become more
human if not empathetic.
All this being said, heavy music,
like the Silver Surfer riding his surfboard
through the universe in search of lush worlds
for the primordial being Galactus to absorb,
conjures and revels in the macabre, and offers
an escape room from the mundane,
spilling crumbs and the other
stains of daily life.

SPEED UP AND OPEN YOUR EYES BEFORE YOU MISS THE SURPRISE

I am a zombie who is separated from his family
I wake up in a pool of sweat from alcohol and strange dreams
Someone is playing a symphony in the apartment
The blood thirst is more distracting than screaming neighbors
and nothing is as it seems
Idiots with guns in lumberjack shirts have lost their sensibility
cannot peer outside their windows to meet the gaze
of the placid dove(s)
I am in a zombie fantasy and your happy insanity
or guns will not help
you flee from me

SIDE II: CONCEPT ALBUM

NEW DIMENSIONS STRADDLE TWO WORLDS

I want to learn a new song about my doppelgangers.
I no longer want to be lost and found with ghosts
in society's terrifying glass castles and digital trash
that poses as balm and fools your brain into thinking you are
lucky or not lucky and so have no control over your daily lives.
In the library
I am not a writer
nor an artist
but a guide
into this world of information
that can punch you in the face.
Make you prostrate, obsessed, distorted
and out of your real body
so hungry for difference, so maligned, so separated
from timeliness and cash streams, lighting strikes of three
that never stop flourishing as you suffer,
are erased/become erasure.
The mortal version of me is made of rice,
peanut butter, neurotic mania.
You will not deliver the other me to me
or anyone else I care about by helicopter.
Will you share your secret language so wild and enduring
and full of illustrations?

THE SUBWAY

The Subway and the
subway cars, one grimy
shiny odorous fascinating
beautiful mosh pit impromptu,
except no one wants to be there
while they are there, especially
when in transit to work, sweaty
jerked this way and more often
fatigued than contemplative as you
block out the world with Air Pods
and metal. In a recent dream your
father was an expressionless centaur
guarding the entrance to the basement.
When he opened the door without the
lights on
It looked like a subway
tunnel with gnashing teeth and burning
orange eyes staring directly at you,
and then you woke up dozing
with the book *Trouble in Mind*
by Lucie Brock-Broido
about to fall out of your hands
as you caught it with a sudden burst
of ancient track team little league reflexes
all before the next transfer.

REAL LIFE

Glue sticks and scissors and pens disappear
as I do when I clean my hands with too much
hand sanitizer and they dry out until they
begin to fade at the library reference desk.
New major winter storms create constant
grocery store line hysteria while I mostly
just shrug shoulders and imagine rolling
big boulders up and down hills.
Smile, there are no genies in the baby's bottle
but within myself. I forget constantly there
is no big money fast or on sale.
Metal, your horns do shine in my ears
like Viking helmets in an opera performance.
I fight old school, which is not at all
about auditioning under golden halos
of power, far and wide.
My guinea pigs have a power dynamic.
One's the Alpha; one's the submissive,
yet they switch roles now and again
sometimes in the same day
and only give a shit about who
wins the spot in the sleeping bag or house
not pushing you off your pedestal
or subverting the status quo.

FAR BEYOND MEMORY

At Nassau Coliseum,
where the Long Islander's hockey team plays,
I saw Pantera with the opener Type-O-Negative
with my friend Anand
and I don't remember who else.
The indelible image plastered to my brains
is lead singer Phil Anselmo
jumping on top of gigantic speakers to start
Pantera's version of a sing-along to "Fucking Hostile."

Life is heavy metal and it is heavy,
always encasing us in its snarling jaws
as the power chords bring us to our knees
or make us soar in the mosh pits.

Life is heavy metal.
As we wake we hear the machine noises from cars and
buses and dishwashers and radios and on our phones
like zombies we touch and stare, as we get ready for work.

Heavy metal is sword and sorcery, or so we are told,
or as it is written.
Heavy metal is don't forget the groceries—

WISHING I MAY HAVE MIGHT

I wish to ride the lightning
and nothing was very very frightening
but nothing is ever the same
when a giant steel-toed boot
kicks you in the head
as you're leaning up against the fence
at a Faith No More concert with the opener Steel Pole Bathtub
and are hauled out of there,
dizzy and out of breath,
a wimp kicked in the head and smelling salts applied
in the tinted orange glow of Roseland Ballroom.
I would like to apologize
to my younger (not less anxious)
yet quicker to heal self.
Like Opera the Metal never leaves your body or mind;
The subway commutes to work
and the atonal machine sounds,
the gritty encounters a kind of mosh pit
you can never escape
even when your headphones are on
listening to the soundtrack of your lives
to block out all distractions.

Puzzles in Hidden Cities

Sleeping giants on subway trains hear voices.
We keep our headphones on, mind our business
in spite of the zombie spells, our phones,
the cracking of psyches, their aching bones.
Where are the mutant turtles floating?
Below the city is ruled by rat kings
who screech laments about their lost
rings of cheese and crocodiles
who charge them the highest fees
for safe entrance through the sewers.
Where garbage is gold to be bartered
while we gnarled humans barely notice,
sometimes even blocking out breakdancers
who flip and jump on the bars above us
to a soundtrack, some of us holding on
for dear life, and we watch them with wonder
and fear we will be kicked in our faces.
Sleeping giants on subway trains see things
and it seems like magic when they can't afford
their meds and all us zombies try to take a pause
on our blood thirst until we get to whatever we
call home. The rat king rides his ship made of
metal cans and candy wrappers on Styrofoam
containers to escape his underlings who have had
enough of his tyranny and are protesting their lack
of wages, hope, freedom and care, the clock that
rings and forces them to keep working like worker
bees to build his kingdom, a maze without a reward
at its ending and through the grates the world
keeps bending…

TOOL POEM #3

There's no invincible being but yet you sing it
probably as a metaphor about our current
slate/state of political leaders, extreme con men
and whores burning into your social media consciousness
like a blunt object to spite their enemies and
keep their supporters in stasis
until all the votes are counted
and they touch all the bases.

The singer sings about extinction including us,
that it doesn't matter if we think we are invincible
or descending into webs of chaos,
because we are not
but it's dangerous ignorance and
will destroy us.
In the arctic nether regions, the survivalist fantasy,
we must fight polar bears and eat their meat
when we should be working to stop
the ice from melting
not breaking more
so we don't vanish
and fall into the
sea.

Them Bones: An Indirect Alice In Chains Tribute

At 1:30 a.m. it sounded like my neighbors
were grinding bones in the sink.
It was like a very old about to break vacuum
ready to cough up its final lung.
I was trying but failing to be in love
not like the giant in Jack and Beanstalk was
about to grind me down to make his bread.
Also, I had just watched one of the final episodes
of Game of Thrones with its epic painful battle scenes
with the dead.
Back to the neighbors; why are they hanging out in the
kitchen until 2 a.m. Cleaning cooking making so much
rattling noise.
My wife is finally asleep. I'm wide-awake listening to them
argue about God knows what
while cooking the next day's dinner?!
Well, it does smell like onions.
I do not know when they stopped,
when they ended their cruel oral
torture, but at some point,
I started to fade into a kind of fitful slumber.
Now, I am trying to shakily write and avoid the
stinging sunshine.

Concept Album

Every, or almost every night my wife
and I drink a glass of red whether
Chianti, Malbec, Merlot or Cabernet Sauvignon.
Red wine is like horror movie blood pools, the
inside of the human body, fury of a frustrated
life rife with endless battles, and many other
symbolic political nonpolitical things that empower
or make the head ring. Is this Heavy Metal? Or romantic
nostalgia driven nonsense like roses and their thorns,
and how the petals descend when they blacken and die.
Heavy Metal is rarely hearts fluttering in the wind,
Hallmark cards unless it's time to make bank and fulfill that
record contract. Heavy Metal can be regal extreme
doom and dirty aggression for aggression's sake,
revolution on the backs of slithering snakes in a
burning field. The witches, warlocks, spaceships
alien war themes are both horror and science fiction,
yes, but the prog-rock album is a dying breed but
bands like Mastodon, Dream Theater, Coheed and
Cambria, maybe a few others, carry the torch of the
mythological time traveler universe and wail it
whether ethereal keyboards or guitar solo heavy.

PERSONIFICATION: EXTINCTION CHRONICLES

Can we make more happen than burning to the ground
and tears?

Become a disappearing collection in the noble library of
noble thoughts and concepts shelved.

Have you ever said you've run out of yourself?

The ego is a regal thing but has no crown.

I am in a rush not to slip into slush on my way to the train
and then the bus.

Are we all repelled by the no longer fresh pond
like we should be?

We should become the dragon fly
sipping the sweetness of our soda.

The paradise of the aquarium and all its colors are in danger.

We are the fish running out of bubbles to breathe.

I'm tired of the wretched and the vile garbage pile left
for the stray animals to scavenge and be poisoned.

I will become a hologram of a dog, a cat or a giraffe
and then go on the hunt for predator or prey.

Can we fake more than ego filled statistics that say
we love you and you and you and not that you vanished
one day under the swamps of decay from which you
came...

There are men and women with black eyes

and in wheelchairs
sleeping on tables and floors in
corners with plastic bags of vodka in hand
gulps accompanied by vile smells of death.

Are you in a desperate state? — Can you fix the broken
record? — Can you recognize yourself in the mirror
before you are slumped over, before the EMTs arrive,
before your pets walk on their hind legs and take you home?

SIDE IIII: INTERROGATIONS

LOBSTER GIRL, I FEEL BAD FOR YOU: A METAL POEM

You are so orange red sunset death
It hurts to look at you
with your friends in the front row of Giants stadium
at the tour headlined by Metallica, Linkin Park and
some math rock band in makeup I cannot remember.
Lobster girl, you should go the hospital not chug watered down
beer until you no longer notice the toxic poisonous glow.
How are you moving?
What brain cells are you losing?
Lobster girl, you are young skinny and addled
and if you could jump in the mosh pit you would
even though you might get kicked and punched,
and wail that you are on fire.

SAD DONUT!

I am going to start a heavy metal band called SAD DONUT! Named after the half eaten pink frosting sprinkled donut I saw on the counter in the Dunkin' Donuts window on my way to my next transfer at 74th and Roosevelt. Our first doom and gloom with a spittoon song will be called "half-eaten donut"

I will scream "all by my lonesome" over and over again while chugging hot black coffee. The song will be about the working-class struggle and the rich who squeeze our resources until they are dry or disappeared. "Sad donut, sad donut" will be another lyric in my cookie cutter death growl. I will howl at the moon instead of barking as a part of the performance.

We will have a half-eaten donut mascot who will also be our bass player that plays with plastic fingers that are not fingers but made of hardened sugar and apprehension who can never pluck only slap.

My Wounds Have a Message, the Toxic Truth Soothsayer

My wounds have a message.
If you see spies
splash water on your eyes
and look again out the window
with binoculars as if at the birds.
If you hear a humming you might
be bugged or not, but do not
worry about the fires to come.
It may be paranoia.
Have a cup of chamomile tea.
The playbook of your worry newsfeed
is constant upsets, not sore
throats and sentences with the
word "death" in them and headlines
continuing to damage hearts and eat
package after package of Life Savers,
your sugar addiction fever no longer
undiagnosed as the poor often are when it's
terminal.

My wounds have a message.
They plead with you to make
top secret friends so that the
contamination can end,
all that is out of whack
technological and political.
I am not contaminated, right?
I am not made out of high fructose corn syrup,
hydrogenated oils, MSG or
(other acronyms turning us a dark orange shade),
too many carbs, the wrong carbs, too much sugar,
not enough sugar, a list of greens I've missed
saying what's the best kind, whether broccoli,
cauliflower, nuts, blueberries or other combos.

My wounds have a message.
They are not saying you will no longer
have a long-ass commute, or super high
energy bills, or neighbor children
who seem to be climbing and banging walls
simultaneously, and keeping their bright lights on
all night in living room and kitchen.
I am not a curator but my accumulated
cuts and burns and scrapes have been told they build
character when I know they are characters,
and get ornery when not stretched out or recognized.
At night, I don't come alive but keep calm if sleepy
during the everyday endless days risking mania and
delirium, even psychosis pushed up against metal poles.
How does fascism work when the improbable fall
and these palaces, these truths we take for granted
vanish as the heartland vanishes.
I haven't recently taken an oath,
yet I'm not a rule maker or breaker or
try not to become transformed or shaped by them.
Sometimes, my mind's microprocessor wishes
I were a puppet or a sculptor or farmable land.

IN THE THEATER OF MY DREAMS

I live in a wall of sound
raining blood and peace
that sells but who's buying
and Chaos (A.D.) that the band
Sepultura became semi-metal
famous for, except now I am on
St. Marks street eating a falafel sandwich
at Mamoun's still relatively cheap,
after or before a poetry reading at the KGB.
I think I remember the poet Billy Collins
was reading just as his fame rose—
I barely could poke my head through the
red doors for a Baltika beer, and
although he's a poetic tumor for some,
he's so metal, so rock'n'roll or
as close as they come, so dry, sarcastic,
asking do you come to these things often
with silence and lucidity? Today I (we) (you)
are in an actual societal extinction event
and do not get to attend live readings or concerts
except in the virtual like Apocalyptica live
from a small town in Finland as I (you)(we)
plot our re-emergences and our exits.

GRAVITAS, AN OVAL SHAPE

We partially shot our windows, our idiot boxes
so we don't see your faces. The crisis game is to wall off the brain.
We make vows we cannot keep about refunding your truths, your votes,
your demonstrations. Apparent suicide not as rare or in rows as you
would think. We are driven by price to innovate using the black market
where we may get burned. Price, driven by the mood swings of the greedy.
We are fatal, a snail smear asking for money-for-now, not now,
not the last of his kind yet. Galactic collision, black hole, Milky Way,
we will be dead long before you are. Nature dictates, plumbs
new depths of rain and snow and meth done in well-lit rooms or
dark alleyways. We should not have Fit-bit fits nor resolutions.
Only bring what's necessary to the sample sale, synthetic drug users
of superhuman strength and delusion (confusion) (contusion).
We are our own biggest lies, flies on the wall, who drink mud
like we drink coffee. Toast, I am, (you are) (we are) toast, tired
of being roasted and captured for less than our elegance and
wild beauty. Hallelujah! We are or can be fireworks who,
frequently going out, need life-
saving money for groceries with zero waste.
In memorials, we talk
about you, all our stressed out asses hanging out,
with our stories of stupid things
stupid patrons said or did at the Reference Desk or Cyber-Center.

THE NON-NON PLACE

Shivers, slivers of past regression with small
grazing birds near a nature sanctuary bay,
words of doom spliced without sugar or spice,
reality untelevised except in your Armageddon
scenario nightmare brain. When you send out
flares, you are not aware of searching for omens,
good, bad or affirmations. Is laughter intended
to terrify the calm for the actual storms peeling
off the poisonous sunburnt flesh developed poolside?
In another city of rampage, no solutions just tears
reshaped yet again, torn lists of victims and survivors
and results in your empathetic brain. A beach is just
another non non-place to be buried when the scourge of
mental illness lights its neverending fires, and this time,
there are no dojos to be found, just the panic suicidal
machinations of a civil service engineer employee.
Do you wake up sweaty in your hothouse sixth floor
apartment and say to yourself like an elitist douchebag
that you are experimental, exponential or extemporaneous
as you laugh, regurgitate SAT words?
Animals should not suffer dread but when on stage does it
because it's a late-night TV comedy parlor trick? What happens
to the sheep when the sheep forgets to blindly follow? How can
they remember the hollow in their heart if it was never there?
They only seem to be glaring at you with their black eyes
pleading for release before they become your sweater factory pet,
or worse. The Rom-Com, a clichéd trope, is a horror show of its
own, endless, faucet of fake honey, the mashed potatoes, fried
chicken, potato chips comfort food of movies that makes you
forget, or that you merely watch due to its clownish implausibility,
separateness from the raw take on your actual reality. I do not require a
silver bullet to calculate the end of your problematic household finances
picking small pleasures to build more force fields around your children,
and if you have them, go on small journeys or distant ones, be frugal,
do not leave, do not break, never go, get an education, find your galaxy's
edge, engage your collective awakenings, fall into it.

INTERROGATIONS OF SELVES

Are you going to touch me?
Are you going to interrupt,
my constitution, inside and out?
What is authentic, beauty?
Are you going
to sail around the world to learn
about all our tribes and
watch the oceans unfurl before
our eyes? Are you going to get off
the couch and stop staring at your phone?
What if I pull the plug or offer a ham
bone soup or a plan, a plain old-fashioned
coup? What is a hitchhiker? Where and who
are our citizens? Life is spectacular or
supposed to be. Have you ever peered through
the telescope during moonlight, like Copernicus,
Galileo and thought of both the mysticism
and the science? If life is a sinkhole are you
watching in a cracked bowl? Are you going to
shoot even if I raise my hands?

Do you want to touch me?
Why are you on top of me,
when my hands are behind
my back while I am on the
ground, when I can't even hear
the breeze? Why does the air sound
like cracking concrete? What is
rumbling at my feet? Can (you) (we)
go beyond wealth to build everyone
a roof and shelves? Do you have memories
of chains in thoughts, pictures, and actions?
Are you going to touch me? Are you a spell?
Can you fell a tree? Can you migrate like a
bird but in the best ship, not treated like cargo
or a prisoner? Are you afraid of my touch?
Are you an absent or an all-too-present-boss?
Do you mistake obsessive passion for mental illness?

How can we know the difference? When all are
serene and unassuming and speak in dulcet tones
and not in shotgun-speak? Are you a recipe?
Do you like to invent your own sauces? Do you
stir and fry? Have parts of earth become more
like Mars? Will we all tragically disappear and
not just in the winds, in the deserts? Are you going
to touch me? Will you continue to interrupt me?
What has happened to our celebrations or
joy? Why is empathy the best medicine
to recover from slumping over in a chair,
a disease bringing you to your knees?
Is life a spelling bee and are we merely winding
down to the finish line not even bothering to take
our temperatures, or should we continue to
follow the sun and seek out the flowers, fruits, the
blood for the planet, even the thrill of defeat,
which should be a learning experience and not on
repeat, not weaponized, like our words. Are you going
to touch me?

SIDE IV: DOCUMENTS

DOCUMENT #15:
THE PRESENT FUTURE PAST

The magician seeks private care and truckloads of ambition.
Crusaders were islands unto themselves until their time ran out.
Did their offensive comments become too offensive or did they embarrass
the powers-that-be, pressured into slaps on the wrists?
Are we lost in dreams of time or puppets hanging from wires?
Big brands don't struggle to resolve fears behind plastic waste.
Is a head on a spike imminent as the shutdown lingers?

The magician seeks private care and truckloads of ambition
not force fields blocking the potency of their potions.
Are we lost in dreams of time or puppets hanging from wires?
Paradise is a simmering campfire about to go inferno.
Transparent drones don't moan and work all night and all day.
They land on tiny desks and ignore cruelty.
Chaos is utterly exhausting for admirers of rare books
about to vanish with the memory of our discoveries.
Are we hyper-allergic and instant and expecting?

The magician seeks private care and truckloads of ambition.
Are we lost in dreams of time or puppets hanging from wires?

DOCUMENT #12: THE DANCE

In childhood dreams, I fell through endless black holes
while listening to late night sports radio and heavy metal tapes.
The jewels rage against machines in their golden bathtubs
as ants protect their hills from being crushed by giants.
The dance acquired at dawn in Babel while hailing Satan
(Hallelujah!)
is a dawn of blood rushing to the head and waking
as we offer up the middle finger to time and
space, its constraints on our/my moods and ambitions.
The jewels rage against machines in their golden bathtubs
who look down on us all that disagree with their
rich or poor and do not bow as if you were on a pedestal.
I wake in darkness to annoying phone alarms.
The dance acquired at dawn in Babel while hailing Satan
(Hallelujah!)
What is it to have dead eyes and do we know it?
The jewels rage against machines in their golden bathtubs.
They think empathy is a social disease to be defied.
The dance acquired at dawn in Babel while hailing Satan
(Hallelujah!)
is not done in downward dog, not a ceremonial drink that brings you
higher.

A Manual for Hope and Nightmares

Does hope have guidelines? I had a dream swinging
on the monkey bars when I slipped because there was
hand sanitizer on the bars. Us friends were on Zoom
last night partying and eating and drinking from a distance;
I know weird, right? Zoom sounds like a super villain
from DC comics made of metal or ice or a bad rip off of
the Flash. Does hope have guidelines? All we have is talk or
silence or ourselves for the moment as we think don't come
any closer, we'd rather not die from an abundance of self-isolating
in apart-ness we could not have imagined. Does hope have guidelines?
Many escapes, a special, multiple split screens and faces in fear and
solitude. What if the ambitious cannot afford experimentation, do not
have Harry Houdini skills of illusion, live in comic strips, want to get
things done, make nice dinners while listening to WSOU Seton Hall
Pirate radio heavy metal to silence to the thoughts to be left behind
as the money vanishes? Does hope have guidelines? Regrettably, the
disease is (us)(our) leaders and not a fantasy; the disease is the ghost of
empathy and compassion, counterfeit facts that foment rage and social
division as our fables become our existence and a kind of containment.

CONFLICTING SIRENS

Sometimes, I wish I could hide in a new empty seltzer box
like my guinea pigs who munch on hay, carrots, other crunchy snacks
and forget the moments where the falcons are coming for me, the
end is always near and forever no matter where we run or hide or
how clever. I'm not there on the frontlines but every day my vision
becomes fuzzier reading story after horrific story and its avalanche
is like heavy metal descending over my head in fifty mile an hour
winds. I'd like to say my wife and I are well and we are and not
relative to the circumstances and the day, what we ate and
who we heard wronged whom outside our winds, if we
remember our dreams/nightmares, a future that looms
instead of rises in exasperation at finally returning to abnormal
and observing the same blazing sun, the same downpours, the
same hungry mouths. Sometimes I wish I could hide
and realize I have always been hiding from myself,
everyone and their conflicting sirens…

DOCUMENT #5: SIGNS OF LIFE (UNSTUCK IN TIME)

Subterfuge is a cloud of smoke sealing the country off from the world
listening to a comedic virtual DJ set helps us forget and unwind.
The inventive chef in higher volume worlds looks for an elixir,
hallucinogenic sauces drizzled on fish, chicken, beef and vegetables.
Whom are we now and does it matter as we come out the other
side of the looking glass?
Farts are signs of life until neighbor babies break down the walls,
shrieking and howling back and forth until they are tired out or
get their way.
Whatever we do we are tired and melancholy as we become more
socially distant.
The inventive chef in a higher volume world looks for an elixir.
In their gardens, turning bitter herbs, roots and weeds into salvation.
Diets go the way of extinction although we are cooking mostly,
not ordering takeout.
Farts are signs of life until the neighbor babies break down the walls
and tear your apartment to shreds as well as your remaining sanity.
Essential workers are being told you are on your own
and we will work you to the bone until your expiration.
The inventive chef in a higher volume world looks for an elixir
in turmeric, in cumin, in coriander, in peanut butter and jelly
in Buddha-like bellies wise as they are full.
The not so silent killer is politician's politics that blatantly do not care
whether we are dead or alive, attack their greed and
turn our smoke to fire…

USED FOR PARTS

The dark chill that comes at the sky
has not been filtered through a BRITA.
My ears itch on the inside, are filled with wax
yet I hear cat baby goat sheep outside my window as the cars splash
back and forth in puddle rivers.
Corporate death remembers letters you used to write and
receive from your grandfather.
Here, swallow this poison called poison.
What do you have to lose, I'm
only trying to kill you; do you understand
the meaning of sacrifice; I'm sacrificing you for the economy.
Men with tiny slit eyes and giant heads,
wide yes, wolf teeth and dead eyes shout: Pollute! Pollute! Pollute!
from the rooftops as they dump all the chemicals into the sea
and do not sigh but voraciously grind their teeth as an endless
flow of cash floods their bank accounts, and erasure.
I need calming music to quiet my manic energy
but also the aggressive music, a live performance.
The dubious will take our votes,
crumble into a ball and start a bonfire
to retighten their control over the power panel switches.
It appears that we are screwed
and only the lowest rungs of society's classes get it in the end,
and are in suspended animation (and not just as a nation).
The death cult wishes for their own death
as if it's liberty, as if only their enemies
will die and the illness is not real
until they are exposed and perish.
We can't pay our bills with money
that doesn't exist poltergeist vulture landlord
zombie vampires; with jobs that are no more,
banks asking for money we do not have.
The hypnotic eye is a jigsaw puzzle
that never wears an eye patch or a muzzle.
I am wearing a hoodie in my apartment
it is so cold and may have to turn off the AC
so my guinea pigs do not freeze their furry butts off.
Just wearing gloves and masks alone will not save us from ruin
as they hit us with blunt metal objects and melt us down or use us for parts.

VIRAL DAYS (DAZE)

Am I hearing a plane swooshing in the air or is it a car or a bus driving through potholes and mud puddles and honking.? This is not a play or a simulation or (merely)(simply)
a living nightmare
or just another dark morning. We all need masks so that we can breathe, and that cover our entire faces as the rain comes down before the curtain comes down, we bow, and are exposed.
Why can't (I)(we) find a (pot dealer) in the (apocalypse) (pandemic)?
I am cooking almost every day as very few restaurants stay open for takeout as more become infected and it becomes riskier, not profitable enough to stay open even our favorite local liquor store has gone home for two weeks.
Heavy Metal is not just jargon, a barrage of speeding
riffage and atonal garbage pail sounds pounded into the brain but a castle in the sky that touches the clouds like our skyscrapers do that were of course built with metal. Heavy Metal is a fist in the air, a warrior cry, a call to arms to protect our fellow human beings, the neverending race against the forces of the devil among us; and this for me, is not simply a matter of seeing through smoke and mirrors but be unable to comprehend what something is when we see or hear it and I'm not talking about what is going viral.
Yesterday, I baked banana bread while my wife set up a Zoom
meeting and made specialized purple drinks, and our guinea pigs screamed Wheek! Wheek!
Because they heard those alluring kitchen noises and wondered what's coming our way, asking, givers of lettuce will save the day?
Are you okay?
—This is not Mad Max, The Terminator,
The Matrix or other end-time films
except some cults who are waiting for the resurrection.
Am I hearing a plane
swooshing in the air, or is it my imagination because our bodies are gone and we are only minds and memories like an archive of lives streaming forever in the digital landscape
in a battle of factions like we are currently
residing in—Is this Heavy Metal?

METAL, HEAVY

If I was writing about the Industrial Revolution, as I did in high
school, what would be more heavy or metal or metal, heavy than
this, as the abused workers fight
for their dignity, their civil rights against
the owners and corporate elites
of the day, and bring us into the modern world
of both skilled and unskilled
assembly line factories, whether making clothing or automobiles
whereas today we barely build anything in America
except unrest in
pieces because of how much it costs;
perhaps microchips microprocessors
for computers and sometimes organic food items
and clothes but rarely
unless we are in our small business building phone covers,
socks or jewelry
on crafting websites.
This poem is becoming an essay as one could
argue Heavy Metal's lineage is connected to artists,
writers like Poe and Baudelaire
so fascinated with the lower classes,
the underpinnings of society as well as the
personal mental illness drug addicted
sordid incident in their own lives
whether as judgmental observer of the peddler,
the thief, the vagabond, the
whore, the animal spirit enigmas
and other paradoxical scenarios and
stereotypical figures painted with a
disturbing morbid fascination with love
and lovers. Metal, heavy, is 9/11,
heaven's crooked stairway, zombie warriors,
wise or trickster skulls, a psychedelic highway,
steel plants of old, dressing up
in leather and studs, fighting the weather's extremes,
manipulating our DNA
and genes to head off or start the apocalypse,
apocalypse, apocalypse as we text
our way to oblivion or fall short of saviors.

DOCUMENT #16: THE FINE LINE OR LIVING IN AMERICA

The Twilight Zone is not made of blueberries
and orange drops. I have broken hands. Have they
become hot and toxic? Are all our pleasures becoming
virtual? Is farm fresh a thing of the past? This is no time
for us or is it for experimental methods except in your
imagination, which will have to now simulate your hopes
and dreams. The Twilight Zone is no longer merely eerie
and hypothetical; its inhabitants on fire, a fire perpetual,
a book of poetry or science fiction novels suddenly predicting
the future where all the dried goods have vanished, and we
become the mask that we are wearing post-isolation. Now the
winds are in the capital and brazenly the power-full is still
shaking hands and molesting microphones and checking off
their oppression of the poor and minority bucket listen while the
colorful flowers try not to perish above them, all in the Rose Garden.
The Twilight Zone is mundane like a pile of empty potato chip bags,
caramel candy bar wrappers, soda cans not filled with soda but vodka;
all the gatherings are beginning to stop; there is no music, people are
not going out because Broadway and all shows are shut down. Will
virtual gatherings become the new norm? Will we all yearn to sit on
wooden, metal or cement benches in the sunshine while the sparrows
bounce around and the weeds bloom in the sidewalk cracks?—

Acknowledgements

The Bowery Gothic: "The Shadow You"

Big Other: "Document #15: The Present Future Past," "My Wounds Have a Message (The Toxic Truth Soothsayer)," "Interrogations of Selves" and "Gravitas, an oval shape. "

Heavy Feather Review: "Personification: Extinction Chronicles"

Poets of Queens Anthology: "Tool Poem #3, "Far Beyond Memory"